ACTIVATING YOUR SPIRIT GUIDES
THE SHAMAN'S WAY

Norman W. Wilson PhD

ACTIVATING YOUR SPIRIT GUIDES
THE SHAMAN'S WAY

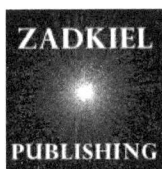

ZADKIEL

PUBLISHING

DISCLAIMER

There are no guarantees that the procedures described herein will work for everyone.

For some, a shaman may be necessary to assist in them in channeling their Spirit Guides. Please note, you may have more than one Spirit Guide.

If you have medical issues check with your physician before attempting any of these procedures.

Persons under the age of eighteen should not attempt these activities.

Within this world of polarity choice and free will, you have an opportunity to realize your full potential as a divine expression of your creator, becoming a creator yourself in the process.
Gregg Braden
Awakening to Zero Point: The Collective Initiation

ACKNOWLEDGMENTS

My many thanks go to my loving wife, Suzanne for her encouragement, understanding, and patience as I worked my manuscript.

I am deeply indebted to Susanna Mantis, aromatherapist, for her help in deciding which essential oils are most likely to aid meditation. She mixed the oils for me so that I could verify their effectiveness. Her website: www.zsremedies.com.

Anna Sundari Knight, an expert in crystals, provided the information on which crystals to use and apply the techniques described in *Activating Your Spirit Guides-the Shaman's Way*.

A Path to Avalon, a metaphysical store, located in Arlington, Washington is an excellent source for crystals. The website is: www.apathtoavalon.com

Dragons With Your Tea located at Stanwood, Washington. It's an excellent source for herbals.

A heart-felt thanks to my publisher, Stuart Holland at Zadkiel Publishing for bringing this book to life.

Author's Note about this Version

After further thought, I felt I needed to revisit *Activating Your Archetypes* and place a greater emphasis on my original intent—activating one's spirit guides. Believing everyone has at least one such guide, I felt more should be said about the value of spirit guides in daily life and to provide additional techniques and information where relevant to my main purpose. As a consequence, I have changed the emphasis in some areas and added new content to others.

CHAPTER ONE

There are two things I have come to believe implicitly about the world we live in. One is that nothing occurring in it is independent of any other thing; the other is that nothing that occurs is entirely random and prey to change.

Allan Combs and Mark Holland
Synchronicity

I invite you to come with me and mind-walk into the fields of science, mythology, psychology, and neuroscience. Meander with me, like on a country path, through some radical forests of ideas. We will occasionally stop by a sparkling brook to absorb a whiff of intoxicating elixirs as they bubble up and out of the well-springs of universal consciousness—a consciousness we are still struggling to understand.

To develop a metaphor, it is necessary to turn to the physical sciences, especially holographic science. Those of you who have visited Disney and gone through the Haunted Mansion have experienced holograms at their finest. Holograms appear on greeting cards, Halloween costumes, book jackets, key chains, business cards, coffee mugs, and wherever else one wants a three-dimensional image.

One of the many things that make holography possible is what is called *interference*. Interference is the crisscrossing pattern that occurs when two or more waves ripple through each other, not unlike the waves of water. If you drop a stone in a still pond, you will notice two sets of waves that expand and pass through one another. It is this complex arrangement of crests and troughs that result from such collisions that are called an interface pattern.

A hologram is an interface, and it is produced when a laser light is split into two separate forms.

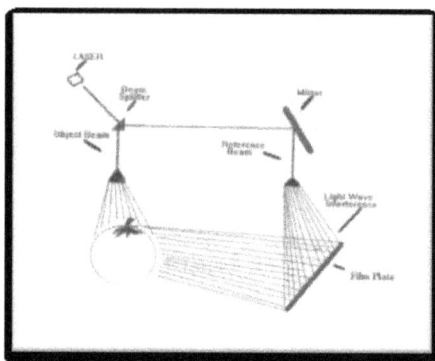

The first beam is bounced off the object (the tomato in the illustration) to be photographed. The second beam is allowed to collide with the reflected light of the first. The resulting interface pattern is then recorded on the holographic film.

If you look at the film, the image will look nothing like the tomato that had been photographed—it would look like the concentric rings that formed when a stone is dropped in a pond. The magic takes place when another laser beam is shone through the film—a three-dimensional image of the original object (the tomato) reappears. This is only one aspect of the holographic marvel. If you cut the film in half and then quarters, each piece will produce a complete image of the tomato. In other words, each fragment contains all the information recorded in the whole. Keep a clear understanding of this in mind because it becomes important in our understanding of the Jungian archetypes and the transition to spirit guides.

Some scientific circles believe this is how our human memories are distributed in the brain as opposed to being localized. For instance, the pineal gland is believed to have a relationship to that distribution. Evidence continues to mount showing vision functioning holographically as well. Holography offers an explanation of how our brains can store so much information.

Physicist John Von Neumann has calculated that over the course of a human's lifespan, a human brain stores 280,000,000,000,000,000,000 bits of information. That's 280 quintillions.

Dr. Paul Reber, professor of psychology at Northwestern University drew the following inferences about the brain's capacity to store information: "The human brain consists of about one billion neurons. Each neuron forms about 1,000 connections to other neurons, amounting to more than a trillion connections. If each neuron could only store a single memory, running out of space would be a problem. You might have only a few gigabytes of storage space, similar to space in an iPad or USB flash drive.

Yet, neurons combine so that each one helps with many memories at a time, exponentially, increasing the brain's memory storage capacity to something closer to around 2.5 petabytes (or a million gigabytes). For comparison, if your brain worked like a digital video recorder in a television, 2.5 petabytes would be enough to hold three million hours of TV shows. You would have to leave the TV running continuously for more than 300 years to use up all that storage." [1]

Holograms, likewise, have a fantastic capacity to store information. Using the holographic approach, a one-inch piece of film can contain the information of 50 Bibles. Being suggested here is the notion that our brains function as holograms and like the hologram, each piece or part of the brain contains the whole image.

The brain with its vast capacity for storing information, functioning as a hologram, then may very well create its own images or pictures. And if, as it is being suggested, all parts of the hologram can create an image and that all parts are related to the whole image as a single entity, we may find that what the ancient mystics have been saying is true—reality is Maya—an illusion. And further, what was out there was really a vast resonating symphony of wave forms transformed into the world as we know it only after it entered our senses. Perhaps the philosopher Immanuel Kant was right after all when he claimed the only way we know is through experience and that is what constitutes reality.

Physicist David Bohm claims everything is part of a continuum—everything is a seamless extension of everything else. Bohm believes that our nearly universal tendency to fragment the world and ignore this very dynamic interconnectedness of all things is responsible for many of our problems scientifically, politically, economically, socially, and psychologically. He does not stop there. He believes that our continued fragmentation of the world not only doesn't work, but it may lead to our extinction.

A classic example of fragmentation is all that encompasses religion. Here's the kicker: Bohm believes that life and intelligence are present not only in all matter, but in energy, space, time, and what we individually abstract out of it. We mistakenly view such an abstraction as separate things. Original people from around the world have long viewed the world as alive. His concept is not unlike that of Mana, [2] which the natives of the Malaysian Archipelago believed. Actually, this is not unlike the early belief in we now call Animism.

This means we are a part and sum of all that has gone on before, and we are interconnected. Advances in DNA analysis strongly support this concept. Not only are we genetically interconnected, but we also contain within our biological entities all knowledge that has existed. Even this notion is not new. Ancient Greek philosopher, Socrates believed that we had more than one soul during our lifetime and that each new soul contained the knowledge of the preceding one. To reproduce this knowledge all one has to do is to ask the right questions. He demonstrated this with an uneducated slave boy. By asking him questions, Socrates showed that the boy knew basic mathematical principles.

The holographic idea also sheds light on the unexplainable linkages that occur between consciousnesses of two or more individuals. Swiss psychiatrist Carl Jung provides helpful insights here. Jung was convinced dreams, fantasies, hallucinations, and artwork often contained symbols and ideas that could not be explained entirely as products of his patients' personal histories. He found that such symbols more closely resembled the images and themes of the world's great mythologies and religions. He concluded dreams, hallucinations, fantasies, myths, and religious visions all sprang from the same source—a collective unconscious that is shared by all human beings.

Jung relates one experience he had with one of his patients in 1906. A young man was suffering from paranoid schizophrenia. As the story goes, one day Jung found the young man standing at a window, staring up at the sun. His head was moving from side to side. When Jung asked him what he was doing, the young man replied he was looking at the sun's penis and when he moved his head from side to side, the sun's penis moved and caused the wind to blow. Several years later, Jung came across a translation of a 2,000 year-old Persian religious text which detailed several rituals and invocations designed to bring on visions. One indicated if a person looked at the sun he would see a tube hanging down from it, and when it moved from side to side, the wind blew.

Furthermore, Jung believes these archetypes were so ancient it's as if each of us has the memory of a two-million-year-old man or woman lurking somewhere in the depths of our unconscious minds. How can that possibly be? An explanation of interconnectedness of all things is predicted by the holographic model. In a universe in which all things are infinitely interconnected, as David Bohm suggests, then it is not unreasonable to have all consciousnesses interconnected. Bohm puts it this way: "Deep down the consciousness of mankind is one." [3]

This meandering country path we are on becomes even more intoxicating when we read what physicist

Fred Alan Wolf says. In 1987, before the annual meeting of the Association for the Study of Dreams, Wolf delivered a speech in which he asserted the holographic model helps explain *lucid dreams*, a type of dream in which the dreamer maintains a full awaking consciousness and is aware that they are dreaming. Wolf reminds us that a piece of the holographic film actually generates two images, a virtual image that appears to be in the space behind the film, and the real image that comes into focus in the space in front of the film. The light waves that compose a virtual image seem to be diverging from an apparent focus or source. This, according to Wolf and others, is an illusion. The real image of a hologram is formed by light waves that are coming to a focus, and *this is not an illusion*. The virtual image of a hologram has no more extension in space than does an image in a mirror. The real image does possess extension in space. Wolf believes that all dreams are internal holograms and that the brain has the ability to generate real images, and that is exactly what we do when we are in a lucid dream or are journeying to another parallel universe.

We just jumped into a fast moving river running along our country path. A gushing river full of eddies, deep holes, shallow pools is more like it.

Wolf then postulates lucid dreams are actually visits to parallel universes. These are smaller holograms within the larger and more inclusive cosmic hologram.

Dr. Paul Davies, a theoretical physicist, and Director of the Beyond Center for Fundamental Concepts in Science at Arizona State University states there are existing parallel universes and in one of them, for example, Richard Nixon is resigning from the presidency of the United States. If Davies is correct, then I suggest Jung's archetypes, these spirit guides or teachers, then, may actually be visits from parallel universes. Is it, for this reason, they are often in the figures of goddesses and gods of bygone millennia? Is this why we see them as ghostly beings and animals? We just made a sharp turn in our gushing river and have plunged into a whirlpool. Take a moment and catch your breath.

Stanislav Grof, a psychiatrist and one of the founders of the field of transpersonal psychology and a pioneering researcher into the use of non-ordinary states of consciousness for purposes of exploring healing and gaining insights into the human psyche, arrives at some conclusions that pale the idea that we are able to access images from the collective unconscious, or visit parallel universes. Grof believes the enfolded nature of space and time in the holographic model explains why transpersonal experiences are not bound by the usual spatial or temporal limitations.

Accordingly, Grof believes the composite nature of archetypal images can be modeled by the holographic idea. Holography makes it possible to build up a sequence of exposures. These composite images represent an exquisite model of a certain type of transpersonal experiences, such as the archetypal images of the cosmic man, woman, mother, martyr, or kore. Grof believes there is a deep link between holographic processes, and the way archetypes are produced. Both he and his wife, Christina, have developed a simple technique for inducing what they call *holotropic* or non-ordinary states of consciousness. The Grofs call their technique *holotropic therapy.*

A second Jungian concept of interest here, is his idea of *synchronicity*—coincidences that are so unusual and meaningful that they can hardly be attributed to chance alone. Each of you has experienced synchronicity at some point in your lives; for example, you have learned a new and different word, and a few hours later you hear it on the radio or television, and then you see it in something you are reading. Jung was convinced such synchronicities were not chance occurrences but were related to the psychological processes of the individuals who experienced them. Jung's problem is this: How an occurrence deep in the psyche could cause an event or events in the physical world. For him, there had to be some new principle unknown to science. He called this the *Acasusal connecting principle.*

Nonlocal connections have been established, and those have given Jung's ideas further credence. Again, Paul Davies states, "These nonlocal effects are indeed a form of synchronicity in the sense that they establish a connection, more precisely a correlation, between events for which any form of causal linkage is forbidden." In other words, these experiences are not based on our normal notions of cause and effect. They are acausal.

F. David Peat, another well-known physicist, also believes the Jungian-type synchronicities are real. He further believes synchronicities reveal the absence of division between the physical world and our inner psychological reality.

Consequently, when we experience a synchronicity, we are really experiencing the human mind operating, at least for that moment, in its true order and extending throughout society and nature, moving through orders of increasing subtlety, reaching past the source of the mind and matter into creativity itself—into the deeper and more fundamental order— the unbroken wholeness of our own unconscious mind.

If then, there is not a division between the mental and physical worlds; these same qualities are also true of objective reality. David Bohm claims the apparent separateness of consciousness and matter is an illusion. If there is no division between mind and matter in the implicate, the ground from which all things spring, then is it not unusual to expect that reality might still be shot through with traces of this deep connectivity.

Take a deep breath. Whew! What does all of this mean? It means from the discovery that consciousness contains the whole of objective reality—the entire history of biological life on the planet, the world's religions and mythologies, and the dynamics of both blood cells and stars—this discovery that the material universe can also contain with its warp and weft the innermost processes of consciousness—that such is the nature of the deep connectivity that exists between all things in a holographic universe.

Archetypal spirits or guides are real, and they help us experience the wholeness that is definitely universally ours. They provide connectivity. Though they may appear to us in various forms such as spirits, goddesses, gods, kindly old men, young children, or animals, archetypes are not myth.

An archetype, according to Swiss psychiatrist and psychoanalyst Carl Jung, is a *preexistent* or latent internally developed pattern of being and behaving, perceiving, and responding. That's certainly a mouthful. By this time our river is overflowing and has tossed us upon a bank of perhaps confused uncertainty. Sit next to the lovely cedar tree, Take a couple of deep breaths. Archetypes are archaic, primordial types with universal images that have existed since the beginning of humanity and they are real!

In this little book, I have tried to establish that archetypes are more than a mere concept, much more. As we progress, hopefully, you will see they are a part of your normal reality and that you can call upon them for help, healing, and or guidance.

Early man called these architypes, spirits. They do appear early in recorded Western history. Philo Judaeus referred to *Image Dei* in man, meaning God-image. This idea is also found in Irenaeus. It appears in the early book, Hermetica. It is in Dionysius, the Areopagite, in St. Augustine as the *idea principales* which is not dissimilar to Plato's *pure forms*. Archetype then is an early paraphrase for ideas relating to the immaterial. Yet, despite the fact archetypes are said to have no material substance; Jung indicates they exist in definite forms in the psyche. Further, they are always present and everywhere. They just don't appear at night. Jung tells us they are "living psychic forces that demand to be taken seriously. . ." [4]

In mythology, these archetypes are called *motifs*. Internationally known anthropologist, Levy-Bruhl called these archetypes *representations collectives*. Two well established authors in the field of religion, Mauss and Hubert, have defined archetypes as *categories of the imagination*. Adolf Bastian has called them *elementary or primordial thoughts*. What then, are the descriptors that have been applied to these inner images, these holograms of the deeper self? They have been called patterns of being or behaving, archaic or primordial, universal images, an unconscious content, God-image in man, immaterial, motifs, and forms in the psyche. Jung tells us that archetypes occur on the ethnological level as myths and they are found in every individual.

The archetype's effect is always strongest, that is, they anthropomorphize reality most, where consciousness is less aware. Jung points out there are mistaken notions that an archetype is determined by its content. That is, it is a kind of an unconscious idea. They are not determined by their content, but only as to form. Such primordial images are determined by their content when they have become conscious and are filled with the material of conscious experience. This is certainly Immanuel Kant's notion once again.

Jung compares the archetype to the axial system of a crystal which performs the crystalline structures in the mother liquid. The archetype itself, like the crystal which comes from its mother liquid, comes from the deep recesses of the psyche—those recesses that connect to the universal collective consciousness—that which is stored in the Akashic Record.

Mythologies' characters are symbolic representations of the whole psyche—the larger and more comprehensive identity that supplies the strength the personal ego lacks. The role ascribed to these mythic characters by Jung is the development of the individual's ego-consciousness—the individual awareness of his or her own strengths and weaknesses—that equip him or her for the many difficult tasks that confront them.

I believe they are much more and as we shake off the confusion created by our bout with this whirlpool of ideas, it will become obvious.

But for now, getting to know these mythic characters existing in your own person becomes even more important in today's society because, and unfortunately so, it is not the human being that counts so much but rather, the function or purpose of that individual, that one differentiated function.

In our modern, technological society, the individual is merely represented by function and what is even more disturbing; we are identifying ourselves completely with function. What I am talking about is a mechanistic world view held by so many in today's cultures; that world view began by Plato, refined by Newton, and made into a palliative by modern media. Take a moment, right now, and think about our mechanistic world.

How many times are you identified by others as well as yourself by function: cashier, attorney, teacher, computer programmer, policeman, truck driver, or secretary? All of these identify function. None tell who you are. Human life cannot, despite the musings of some behavioral psychologists and neuroscientists, be reduced to a machine. A machine is created for a specific purpose, and that is its essential aspect. Human beings do not fit this world of mechanical being.

Today, the study of archetypes and the myths through which they are represented is one way to bring human potential to fulfillment, to put each of you in touch with your inner souls or selves—to connect with your spirit guides. Life and living that life to its fullest is not the function of your existence—it is your existence! However, I must caution you here. The role of myth in archetypal psychology is not to provide an exhaustive catalog of possible behaviors or to circumscribe the forms of transpersonal energies, but rather, it is to open imaginative reflection. As world-renowned Jungian psychologists, James Hillman puts it this way: "Learning about the Greek gods and goddesses can help you better understand who and what is acting deep within your psyches."

Myth has been described as "the dramatic representation of our deepest instinctual life—capable of many configurations, upon which all particular opinions and attitudes depend." [5] As I pointed out earlier, this embodies the leit motif, the archetype, upon which passions, feelings, motivations, attitudes, and beliefs are expressed. We each have a personal myth, a "constellation of beliefs, feelings, and images that are organized around a core, then addresses one of the domains within which mythology traditionally functions." [6] Joseph Campbell lists the following four functions of myth:

1. The urge to comprehend the natural world in a meaningful way
2. To search for a marked pathway through the succeeding epochs of human life
3. The need to establish secure and fulfilling relationships within a community, and
4. The longing to know one's part in the vast wonder and mystery of the cosmos. [7]

My primary interest here is with functions numbers two and four. It is within these areas, we will concentrate our efforts to activate the personal archetype—to connect with our spirit guides.

Activating your personal spirit guide will help explain the world, guide your personal development, address itself to your spiritual longings, your creative and social desires, and it will help provide a sense of social direction. With your archetypal spirit guide is the wisdom of all creation.

There are four basic steps to help you activate your archetype. Within these four steps are multiple levels of instruction. The first step is for you to achieve a relaxed state of body and mind. The second step is achieving a focused concentrated state of mind. Step three is meeting your archetypal spirit guide and step four is releasing that guide. [8]

Each of these steps is to be carefully followed if you want to succeed in activating your archetypal spirit guide(s). I urge you to be patient. Small clues will be given you. Tune in. Let our imaginary river roll on, catch the breezes, and let the sun warm you.

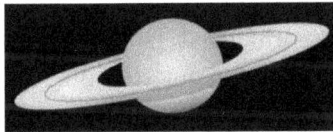

You can alter your state of consciousness without the use of drugs and enter the non-ordinary reality of the shaman. In this state, one acquires firsthand knowledge of a hidden universe.
Michael Harner
The Way of the Shaman

CHAPTER TWO

STEP ONE

Achieving a relaxed state of body and mind is an absolute necessity. Failure to achieve a calm and relaxed state will deny you a connection to your spirit guides. There are several methods to achieve a relaxed body and mind. At no time are you to use any drugs or other stimulants such as alcohol or marijuana. The goal is to create a natural calm resonance.

Go to a room that can be darkened or one in which the light may be lowered. Sit in a comfortable chair or lay down. If your clothes are tight, loosen them. Listen to your favorite song or instrumental piece as long as it is calming. Let your thoughts come and go. Don't linger on any one thought, that is, don't develop it into a scenario. You may want to quietly repeat "um" whenever you start to develop a thought.

Meditate for fifteen minutes every day for two weeks. It may be convenient to do this just before retiring. If so, you may fall asleep. That's fine; don't worry about it. What is important is consistency.

If a darkened room doesn't appeal to you, try a slow, leisurely walk early in the morning or just at sunset. As you walk along, listen to the sounds, note their directions, taste the smells, stop and look around. Breathe deeply, holding your breath and slowly exhale. Do not listen to music through a headset. There is a second purpose to this approach and that is to help you tune into the world around you and ultimately tuning into the Universe.

When you return from your walk, sit down for a few minutes, and let your mind wander about what you saw, heard, and or smelled. Breathe slowly and evenly.

If walking is not your thing, choose and use a relaxation tape, CD, or an MP3. There are a number of very well done recordings available. Some computer software provides intricate designs for your watching pleasure. The purpose here is to learn how to relax. Downing a couple of martinis before dinner is not recommended for the intended purposes outlined here.

Doing breathing exercises is another way to calm your body and mind. Deep breathing means taking a large quantity of air into the lungs, holding it for the count of five, and slowly exhaling through a slightly open mouth. You may shape your mouth into a small round opening to slowly blow the air out, making the sound of the wind.

Or you may choose to make what is called the ocean sound as you exhale with your mouth slightly more open and rounded. to do this, place your tongue gently behind your upper front teeth and blow outward with just enough force so you feel a slight vibration of your tongue against those teeth. As you master a comfortable breathing approach, you should extend the length of time you hold the air in. The goal here is to hold your breath for fifteen to twenty seconds before exhaling.

Another relaxation technique is to lie down and close your eyes. Relax your whole body, beginning with your toes, legs, arms, neck, shoulders, and on through your body. Fill your lungs with air; hold your breath as long as it is comfortable to do so. Exhale slowly, emptying your lungs of as much air as you can. Do this five times. Once this is completed, breathe in;

hold your breath and slowly count from five to zero. As you relax, imagine a glowing soft white light surrounding you. Let it enlarge until it bathes you in its gentle warmth. Then slowly let the light grow smaller until it disappears. This is most effective in a darkened or dimly lighted room.

Once this exercise is completed, return to your normal breathing pattern, keeping your eyes closed. Let your mind wander at will. Wait a couple of minutes and then slowly get up. Be sure to wiggle your feet and toes before attempting to walk. Always be careful.

STEP TWO

Developing a concentrated state of mind is the second step in activating your archetype. It may appear to be a contradiction to ask for a relaxed mind and body and then ask for a concentrated state of mind. It is not. The first is necessary to achieve the second. As in achieving a relaxed mind, there are several available techniques to develop a concentrated state of mind. Admittedly, this borderlines self-hypnosis and should not be undertaken while driving or operating any power equipment. Second, do not try this with a lighted candle because of a potential fire hazard. This is not a game of macho stamina. It is an exercise in concentration.

For this step, you will need the following items: a straight-back chair, a table, and a battery operated candle. There are battery candles with a flickering flame. I use this type of candle and recommend it.

Dim the lights in the room. Do not face a window. If you do, close the blinds and or pull the curtains shut. You don't want distractions. Speaking of distractions, turn of the cell phone, the television, radio, and unplug your earbuds.

Sit straight in the chair facing the candle. Go through one of the breathing techniques described in Step One. Once you have relaxed, turn on the candle. Cup your hands in your lap. Look at the flickering candle light. If you blink your eyes don't worry about it. Keep your mind clear.

As you stare at the lighted candle, repeat over and over the sound OM, dragging it out. Repeat slowly, keeping the sound in sync with your breathing. Do this for fifteen minutes.

Turn off the candle. Sit for a couple of minutes, rotate your feet back and forth, and rub your hands together, vigorously. Then slowly get up from the chair, turn on the lights, open the blinds and or curtains. Move about carefully. Always be mindful of your personal safety.

Do not be discouraged if you don't feel you have succeeded. Practice is essential. Daily practice is necessary. You have to be willing to make a commitment and keep it. You can't operate on the "I don't have time today. I'll do it twice as long tomorrow." If you do, you are courting failure.

Some practitioners of meditation find certain essential oils helpful in quieting their minds and in focusing. Essential oils and their uses go back several thousand years. These oils are called volatile oils or essences. Essential comes from the word quintessence, meaning drawn out of, thus, the principal identifying characteristics of the plant is removed.

It was in 1928 that Dr. Rene-Maurice Gattefose used the term aromatherapy, and it has stuck. Unfortunately, many people associate aromatherapy only with bath lotions, scents for diffusers, and sachets for closets and dresser drawers. Aromatherapy is so much more. It is primarily for healing both physical and emotional pain rather than just a room deodorizer.

For calming the mind, I recommend the following essential oils: English lavender, German chamomile, and frankincense.

USING ENGLISH LAVENDER

Using a mix of English Lavender and jojoba oil, apply two drops in the palm of your hand and rub your hands gently together. Next, cup your hands and hold them close to your nose. Slowly inhale the aroma, drawing in its wonderful smell. Do this five times or more as needed to influence your amygdala gland [9] in your brain. Then rub two drops on the bottom of each foot, and two drops at each temple. As an aside, it takes one acre of lavender plants to create 12 to 18 pounds of vegetation to be distilled into pure lavender oil.

USING GERMAN CHAMOMILES

Like English Lavender, German Chamomile essential oil has a calming effect on the mind as well as the body. Follow the same steps suggested for the use of English Lavender. Like other essential oils, chamomile is obtained from flowers. One pound will yield a dram of oil. Chamomile Essential Oil may be applied directly to the skin. However, some aroma therapists recommend mixing the chamomile oil with jojoba oil. To determine the right mixture consult a certified aroma therapist. And don't hesitate to ask to see the certification.

USING FRANKINCENSE

The sweet aroma of frankincense stimulates and elevates the mind. It will help you in visualizing and improving your spiritual connections. Its comforting properties help you to focus your mind and overcome those daily stresses. Unlike lavender and chamomile, frankincense does not come from plant leaves or flowers; it is derived from the hardened gum of the frankincense tree which is then distilled.

Frankincense comes from Oman, Yemen, the Horn of Africa including Somalia and Ethiopia.

Place two drops of frankincense essential oil on the bottom of each foot and two drops on each wrist. Rub the feet together and then your wrists.

To help you focus, once you have calmed your mind, I recommend the following powerful essential oils: rosemary, juniper, or rosewood.

USING ROSEMARY

Many of you are familiar with rosemary as a spice for food, especially roast beef and certain soups. Rosemary is an evergreen shrub with needle-like leaves and pale blue flowers. It grows throughout Europe, North Africa, the Middle East, and the United States. It has a strong aroma and is widely used for medicinal purposes. Like many of the herbs, it has been used for centuries by cultures around the world. It has been used in weddings, religious ceremonies, used to purify, to heal, and for good luck.

Its essence was first distilled in the 13th century. One of its more important uses is as a tonic for the body's *yang energy* and the promotion of *Qi-energy*. [10] Because it helps boost confidence, it is a natural to help you focus. As with all herbals, there is a caution. Women should not use rosemary essential oil if pregnant or breast feeding. Further, it should not be used on children two years old or younger.

A two percent dilution is recommended.

Place two drops behind each ear and at the top tip of the brain stem. Gently massage it into the skin.

A study, reported in the International Journal of Neuroscience in 2003, suggests rosemary essential oil may help improve brain function. There were 144 volunteers in this small study. Its findings provide a base for further study on the effects of rosemary essential oil.

USING JUNIPER

Juniper, when made into an essential oil keeps its crisp piney smell. There are several dozen species of junipers. The berries of the common juniper are used in medicine, spices, and essential oils.

The juniper is a prickly evergreen that grows to about 39 feet in height and has blue-green needle-like leaves, greenish-yellow flowers, and berries. It helps energize and psychologically cleanse. That is, juniper consolidates one's will-power, thus enhancing the ability to focus. It also has the potential for a deep fortification of bodily functions. To achieve the most benefit from juniper essential oil place two drops on the bottom of each foot and gently rub it in. To increase its potential benefit, place a drop on one wrist and gently rub it in. Generally speaking, it takes only twenty seconds for essential oils to be absorbed into your system.

USING ROSEWOOD

Rosewood essential oil will serve as an example for the country of origin making difference. Rosewood essential oil from Brazil, for example, is more pungent, and on the acidic side while the Rosewood essential oil from Peru is warm and has a floral smell with just a hint of spice. It is extracted from the wood chips of the Rosewood, an evergreen tree with red-hued bark and yellow blossoms.

This delightful oil is uplifting and rejuvenating. Unlike some of the other essential oils, I have suggested, rosewood is not used as a food additive. I recommend you use a diffuser and waft its pleasant aroma toward your nose, breathing in easily to give the olfactory nerves a change to stimulate your brain waves; thus allowing you to be more focused. Mix five to seven drops of rosewood essential oil into water and place that in your diffuser.

Remember, practice is necessary. Do not be alarmed if it takes some time to become effective. Your aim or goal is not getting through the exercises but in doing them well, making them second nature to you. Use the essential oils three times a week. If those I have suggested do not appeal to you, check with an aroma therapist for further suggestions.

Once you understand who you are, the universe will unfold its secrets to you. The wisdom you seek will be yours.

Gautama Chopra
Child of the Dawn

CHAPTER THREE

Our third steep involves meeting your archetypal spirit guide. According to Carl Jung, the archetype has a dual aspect; that is, it exists in both the psyche and in the world at large. In *The Archetypes and the Collective Unconscious* Jung states, "The archetype of spirit in the shape of a man, hobgoblin, or animal always appears in situations where insight, understanding, good advice, determination, planning, etc., are needed but cannot be mustered on one's own resources. The archetype compensates this state of spiritual deficiency by contents designed to fill the gap."

This, I believe, is the same as calling upon the spirit world and this is what a shaman does. Furthermore, Jung suggests that archetypal structures govern the behavior of all living organisms as well as inorganic matter, and they are contiguous with a bridge to matter in general. [11] Many native peoples around the world believe that all things are alive and are governed by the *spirit world*.

This is referenced as *mana*, that is, a supernatural life force. Note the contemporary effort at mapping the DNA of the people of the world is a scientific effort to demonstrate we are all connected. The phrase "One is all-All is one" brings emphasis to that interconnectivity. And that includes the spirit world.

There are four major archetypes:

1. The Self represents the unification of the consciousness and unconsciousness into an individual. Jung often represented the Self as a square, a circle, or as a mandala.

2. The Shadow, existing as a part of the unconscious mind, consists of repressed ideas, fears, weaknesses, and in general, shortcomings. The shadow may appear as a snake, dragon, witch, or sorcerer.

3. The Anima or animus represents the female aspects of the male and the male aspects of the female. Usually, they are considered the true self. What is significant here is the fact that they are a main source for communication with the collective unconscious.

4. The Persona is that image we present to the world; the interaction with social groups, business associates, friends, and family. Like the other major archetypes, the Persona may take on any number of images.

There are many archetypes. Among these are the very familiar father, the mother, the child, the wise old man, the young girl, the hero, and the trickster. Experience dictates the appearance of an archetypal spirit guide may and can take many forms. Dr. Jean Shinoda Bolen reminds us that "archetypes are powerful predispositions; garbed in the image of the mythology of Greek gods—each having characteristics, drives, emotions, and needs that shape personality." [12]

From my perspective these archetypes are not necessarily in the form of Roman and Greek gods. For instance we may encounter images of a deceased loved one or a historical personage may appear. Animals are also frequent visitors, usually representing a specific quality such as courage, all-seeing, cunning, or wisdom. If the archetypal spirit appears as a jester laugh along with him, and then look for the meaning behind the communication he brings. When you meet your spirit guide be sure to say 'welcome.' Always be polite and never be demanding.

I need to digress here for a moment. Demanding is different from commanding. You may command when dealing with the Spirit World. Voice tone sets the stage. Demand indicates something claimed as being due; whereas, command means to direct authoritatively. Being authoritative does not mean you are aggressive.

In preparation for the arrival of your archetypal spirit, you need to activate your pineal gland. Often called the Third Eye, the Eye of Horus, or the Seat of the Soul, the pineal gland is a small pinecone shaped organ inside the brain. It secretes hormones such as melatonin, serotonin, and Dimethyltryptamine. Each of these hormones has specific functions or jobs: melatonin and serotonin are responsible for sleep and for one's meditative state. Dimethyltryptamine is responsible for time dilation, time travel, and journeys to other realms where archetypal spiritual beings are encountered. It is obvious why it is essential to activate the pineal gland if you want to encounter your spirit guide. It is your spiritual bridge between the physical and spirit-worlds.

There are four steps to activating your pineal gland.

STEP ONE – FLUORIDE

What I am about to say may cause some serious debate, but I feel it is essential in order to bring about a positive experience in activating your pineal gland.

Fluoride is a major problem. In small doses, it is harmless, but in today's culture, we are saturated with it: Fluoride is in our drinking water (an estimated 70% of the drinking water in the United States is fluoridated),it's in our toothpaste, and we have fluoride treatments at our dentists.

There are two types of fluoride: calcium and sodium. Of the two, sodium is the most damaging. Sodium fluoride is created as a synthetic waste byproduct from fertilizer, aluminum, and nuclear industries. According to Dr. Josh Axe, sodium fluoride is "already laden with lead, aluminum, and cadmium, and it can combine with other toxic materials to increase their potency. [13] In case you didn't know, fluoride is an active ingredient in rat poison. Yes, I wrote rat poison.

Fluorides have been found to weaken the immune system and other major organs. Once in the brain, it can calcify the pineal gland. Reducing the fluoride level in your body is essential if you are to be successful in activating your Spirit Guides.

There are several things you can do to reduce the negative impact of fluoride on the body and especially the pineal gland.

First, reduce your intake by using non-fluoride toothpaste (baking soda is a good one), non-fluoride mouthwash, suspend or decline the fluoride treatments at your dentist.

Next, drink purified, filtered water, (bottled water may contain fluoride), avoid sodas, juice drinks, and processed foods. Go organic as much as possible. Here is a huge surprise. Do not cook with non-stick pans. Drink white tea or herbal teas. Avoid taking calcium supplements. Most of the calcium is not absorbed in the bones of your body. It tends to clog your internal organs, including the pineal gland.

STEP TWO - CLEANSING

Cleansing the body of accumulated fluoride is relatively easy. Tamarind paste may be used to help decalcify the pineal gland. Tamarind paste is made from the fruit of a tamarind tree. It is sticky and sour tasting. It is used in foods, especially Thai and Mexican cuisines. Good old fashioned Borax is an excellent antidote to the fluoride problem. Simply mix one teaspoon of borax in one liter of water. This may be drunk in small quantities throughout the day.

Cleansing the liver is important. Doing so will rid it of heavy metals and numerous toxins, including the mischievous fluoride. Check with your family physician about cleansing your liver as well as your colon.

A sauna is a pleasant way to remove toxins from your body. Participating in a sweat lodge ceremony is also helpful. If you do participate in a sweat lodge be sure to stay hydrated and wipe yourself down so the toxins are not reabsorbed by your skin. Definitely, check with your doctor before participating in a sweat lodge and make sure those who are providing the sweat lodge are qualified to do so. People have become critically ill and even died in an inappropriate sweat lodge.

Of course eating healthy and avoiding junk foods and sugar will also enhance your wellbeing.

STEP THREE - CRYSTALS

Certain crystals may be used as a cleanser of fluorides and other negative elements that are in the pineal gland. Crystals have been used for thousands of years in a wide variety of healing and spiritual processes. Each person has a power crystal that is unique to them. It is often recommended that a crystal that attracts you is generally your power crystal. You may also visit a healer who will help you determine which crystal is yours.

One of the more powerful cleansing crystals is Sodalite. Sodalite is a member of the group that includes hauyne, nosean, luzurite, and tugtupite. It is a rich blue crystal with a white line of striation through it. Lay down, place a piece of Sodalite on your forehead, close your eyes, and rest for fifteen minutes. Don't hesitate to stroke the crystal, rub it with your thumb and finger. Carry a piece of Sodalite with you. Some have the crystal made into a pocket piece or a pendant to wear around the neck. It can be mounted in a ring.

Clear quartz is another good cleaner. If you don't want to carry a piece of crystal around with you, or wear it, place several pieces of clear quartz around your bedroom, especially on your night stand. As with essential oils, the use of crystals will require time before you see results.

In addition to their cleansing qualities, certain crystals help in contacting your archetypal spirit guides. One such crystal is Chrysocolla, a blue-green stone coming from Israel, Chile, Republic of Congo, England, and the United States. Blue Tourmaline, a very powerful crystal, accelerates the psychic and channeling abilities. It comes from Brazil, Sri Lanka, Kenya and the United States. Black Tourmaline is an excellent stone for protection. If you are planning to journey, black tourmaline is a good stone to have on your person or nearby. Not all spirits are friendly and may inclined to do some mischief.

Creating a crystal grid is helpful in that it brings a concentration of crystals together. It is not necessary to create an elaborate grid. Grids consist of crystals placed in concise, geometric arrangements in order to affect the flow of energy for a specific purpose. "The properties of the stones used, combined with their arrangement in a sacred geometric configuration, creates a unique energy frequency that can be used to enhance your intention and manifest your desired result." [14]

On the next page is an example of a crystal grid designed to activate my spirit guide. In creating your own grid, do not hesitate to use different crystals as long as they mesh with your intention. The intention here is to call up your spirit guide. The crystals I used are Chrysocolla at the West, Blue Tourmaline at the North, Selenite in the center, Labradorite at the East, and Black Tourmaline at the South. See the photo on the next page.

In selecting your crystals for you spirit guide grid make sure those crystals resonate with you. Test each one as you say your intention. If you feel a slight vibration or pulsing, or warmth that is a strong indication that you should use that crystal.

Crystal Grid to Activate Spirit Guide

STEP FOUR - MEDITATION

Meditation serves many objectives, calming the mind, creating a sense of peacefulness, promoting body healing, and providing a means through which one may connect to his or her archetypal spirits. The following techniques are designed to help you connect with your Spirit Guides.

The two forms of meditation are contemplative and concentration. In contemplative mediation, one investigates the object of meditation by thinking about it in detail. In concentration meditation, the purpose is to focus on one aspect of a stated objective; that is, do not let the mind wander.

In Buddhist teachings, this involves what is called single-pointed concentration. It is powerful and effective. You must make every effort to be consistent in your practice. According to neuroscientist Mario Beauregard, "it is interesting to note that a number of neuroscientific studies performed in recent years have demonstrated willful attention and its training through the practice of meditation can lead to important plastic changes in the brain." [15] Richard Davidson's study found "activation in brain regions normally implicated in sustained attention was generally more robust for expert meditator compared to novices. [16] The main point here, again, is practice and dedicated practice is essential.

There are a number of meditations you can practice to help you target your pineal gland. These you should first master before going into other meditative areas. Eden Shetiyah suggests meditating with the word *love*. [17] I prefer the Navajo phrase *Yeha-Noha* which means wishes for happiness. [18] Whichever word or phrase you select, say it to yourself silently. If you don't care for the two suggestions of love or Yeha-Noha consider the traditional *OM* sound.

In a dimly lighted room, sit with back straight in the lotus position. You may sit on a pillow or bolster. If sitting in the lotus position is difficult for you, sit in a chair. Close your eyes. Take a deep breath, holding it a count of five before exhaling. Gently blow out through your mouth. Do this five times. For some, seven times is more effective.

Next, place your left hand's palm

facing up in your lap. Place your right hand on top of your left hand so that both palms are facing up as shown in the illustration. The purpose of this hands

position is to help you develop

consciousness and manifestation. The hands act as a reciprocal and then reflects back to the heart and crown chakras.

Remember, if you are not comfortable sitting in the lotus position try sitting on a pillow or a yoga block. This will relieve some of the pressure. You may also sit in a straight-back chair, feet flat on the floor and just slightly apart. If you are uncomfortable that discomfort becomes a distraction to your meditation.

A slight variation may be more to your liking. Take five more deep breaths, holding each for the count of five. Place your tongue gently between your teeth. Push the air out through your teeth. You should feel a slight vibration on your tongue. As you do this, think of the word or phrase you chose: love, Yeha-Noha, or OM. Do this twice more.

Practice this every day and if you can practice several times a day. Build this time practicing mediation to ten minutes a day. While you are meditating notice how you feel. Do you feel warm, cool? Which parts of your body are you most aware? This is called *cultivating awareness of the present moment.* Note any sounds or smells you experienced. As you continue your practice, you should begin to feel serene. Gradually, increase your meditation to 20 minutes a day. Ideally, thirty minutes should be your goal.

You may complain about the time suggested. As I have said, and have repeated, it requires a commitment. Get up a half hour earlier in the morning so you have time to yourself. You will feel refreshed and energized. If it's more convenient, give yourself a half hour before bedtime. You will sleep better.

Here are some tips to keep in mind as you practice this mediation. Never slouch; always sit straight. Slouching encumbers your breathing and intake of vital oxygen. Close your eyes and take a few minutes to visualize each part of your body; work your way up from your toes to the top of your head. Still yourself and as you quiet down, notice your environment, sounds, smells, colors. Do not, and I repeat, do not try to change anything. All you want to do here is to be aware. Breathe deeply, that is, fill your lungs, hold it for the count of five, and then quietly exhale through your nose or as suggested above. Do not expect your mind to go blank. As thoughts come and go, do not dwell on any particular one. Allow them to float on by.

Once your meditation time is up, don't just stand up. Take a few moments to become aware of your surroundings. Wiggle your fingers, feet, move your arms and legs. Slowly get up from your seated position. Here is a tip for getting up. If you are in the lotus position, slowly unfold your legs, stretch them out in front of you and shake them. Roll over on either your left or right side. Using your strongest leg, slowly push your way up to a standing position. Then as we say in my yoga class, "Shake your booty."

Proper breathing is absolutely essential in the activation of your archetype. One breathing technique has been suggested above. Another approach is to breathe through your nose, making sure you are expanding your diaphragm and not your chest. This forces the lungs to stretch. Work your way up to ten deep, slow breaths per minute and do this for ten minutes a day. Gradually, as you practice this, you should notice a reduction in your heart rate and your blood pressure. Both are an added benefit in your overall preparation to engage your archetypal spirit.

Another breathing technique is to inhale through the nose and exhale through the mouth. Form your mouth into a round shape, and as you exhale make the sound of the wind or as some practitioners say, the sound of the ocean. Fill your lungs, hold it for the count of five, and expel the air through your open mouth.

Music and or sound can play a significant role in meditation. Some experts in the field of meditation claim music or binaural sound is actually a distraction and do little if anything to enhance the meditative experience. I do prefer to use music or binaural sounds. For meditative purposes, a soft, serene music is recommended, no rock, metal, or hip hop. The use of music is two-fold, to set the mood and to calm the mind; that is, it serves as an aid in bringing the activities of the mind under control and thus enabling concentration. Some meditation experts recommend spiritual music, holy chants or hymns. Music acts as a barrier against distraction. Please, no elevator music or the blaring music of some eateries.

Place your source of music within easy listening range. You do not want it blaring in your face, nor do you want to strain to hear it. Listen to the music for a few minutes before actually beginning your meditation. The music should be long enough in duration to provide you 20 to 30 minutes of playing time, enough to meditate.

A brief word about New Age music's appropriateness. It is fine for relaxing. I do not recommend it for deep meditation. It's just too entertaining. Music created for deep meditation is based on the basic principles of psychoacoustics and is designed to take you beyond mere relaxing. They are designed to absorb your attention and clear your mind of noise and idle chatter.

Even though a set of headphones is not necessary, their use is recommended to make the music more personal. Additionally, they do help block out external noise that could be a distraction.

Man is an individual manifestation of all the functions, powers, and affinities in the universe, and his consciousness is the measure of his individualization, his power to make actual that which is only virtual in cosmic harmony.

Isha De Lubicz Schwaller
The Opening of the Way

CHAPTER FOUR

Visualization is the ability to hold an image in your mind's eye. We are born with the ability or skill to visualize and like many of our abilities, it has become dormant. According to Dr. Daniel Kadish [19] "everyone can use imagery to prepare for all kinds of situations. . ." And that, I believe, includes activating your archetypal spirit guide.

Once you have mastered proper breathing, found the right music, and cleared all negative or conflicting vibrations, you are now ready for visualization—the final mastery before unleashing your archetypal spirit guide. Like breathing and meditating, visualization takes practice. Visualization when combined with meditation, and focused breathing techniques enhances consciousness. It brings positive energy to you, the whole you. As your expertise grows, you will be able to tap into visualization at any time you wish. Just don't do it while you are driving or operating machinery of any kind.

The following three exercises are designed to develop your visualization technique.

EXERCISE ONE

Get comfortable, meditate, and breathe deeply. Once your mind is calm, close your eyes and think of a square. Get a clear image of that square. Open your eyes. Close your eyes and visualize the square again. Practice this five times. Next, visualize a circle and then a triangle. After you practice each of these and you are satisfied, visualize the first letter of the alphabet. Are you seeing an upper case or a lower case "a"? Do this for the next three letters in the alphabet. Do this exercise every day for two weeks. At the end of the second week, try to visualize your office or a room in your home. Look at the furnishings? Take your time. If you can't visualize this room, don't panic. Wait a couple of days and then begin this exercise over again. Be patient.

EXERCISE TWO

Place a small vase on a table. If you don't have a vase use any small object such as a box, cup, book, an addressed envelope. Remove everything else from the table. Sit down in a straight-back chair, opposite the vase or object. Look at it, carefully. Notice any details about the vase. Pay attention to color, shape, and nicks, stains, or crackle marks. Close your eyes. Reach out and pick up the vase. Feel of it. Keeping your eyes closed; remove the vase from the table. Open your eyes, and look at the exact spot where the vase had been on your table. Visualize the vase as if it were still on your table.

Practice this until you are comfortable visualizing other objects. Go back and do the latter part of Exercise One.

EXERCISE THREE

Have a notebook or sheet of paper and pencil or pen nearby. Sit in a dimly lighted room, get comfortable and loosen any clothing that is too tight. Turn on your mediation music. Close your eyes. Breathe in; hold it to the count of five. Do this three times. Keep your eyes closed and visualize what your archetypal spirit guide looks like. Is your guide female or male? Look for a head shot as opposed to a full body image.

The image may be somewhat out of focus or it may appear and disappear quickly. That's acceptable. As soon as you are aware of the image say, "Welcome. Thank you for visiting me."

Stay still and listen for a few seconds even if the image is no longer visual. You may sense a message. Accept it. End your session. Immediately jot down what you saw, heard, or felt. Include the date and time and how long your session lasted.

Visitors frequently appear for just a short time and they do this as a test. They want to know if you really summoned them, if you are sincere in your quest, and if you have a question. Notice the word question is singular. Do not approach the archetypal spirit with a montage of questions. If you are seeking help with a specific issue, deal with just that. You can always go back with another question at another session.

The sense of identity expands far beyond the narrow confines of the mind and body and embraces the entire cosmos.
Ken Wilber
No Boundary

CHAPTER FIVE

When you meet your archetypal spirit, you may be in dream time. Using Lucid Dream techniques you can exert some control over the dream. That does not mean your spirit visitor.

At some point, during this experience, you may move into an alternate reality. Sometimes the term parallel universe is interchanged with the term alternate reality. Generally speaking, an alternate reality is a separate reality coexisting with your own and is often considered a variant of your own reality. I prefer the term parallel universe because it allows a broader implication.

The idea of parallel universes is not new. In 1954, Hugh Everett, III, a young doctoral candidate at Princeton University proposed such a radical idea as parallel universes. He claimed there are parallel universes exactly like our own. In one of those, you also exist.

Michio Kaku shares a similar notion when he writes, "particle physics states there is a finite probability for unlikely events to occur such as parallel universes." [20]

Michael Talbot hit the nail on the head when he stated, "In a universe in which all things are infinitely interconnected, all consciousnesses are also interconnected." [21]

Therefore, as you connect with your archetypal spirit, you are connecting with that aspect of universal consciousness entailing all consciousness including that essence that started it all. David Bohm claims that "deep down the consciousness of mankind is one. [22]

Stop, take a breath, and think about this. All is one; One is all. And so we are!

Swedish-American cosmologist, Max Tegmark in an article published in Scientific American (May 2003) titled, "Parallel Universes" claims there are other universes in which there is another person living an identical life to your own. This MIT professor is serious. He states, "The idea of such an alter-ego seems strange and implausible, but it looks as if we will just have to live with it because it is supported by astronomical observations."

From my perspective, this is not all that phenomenal. History demonstrates the existence of others. We call them archetypes or archetypal spirits and when we activate them; we are calling them forth from another dimension or parallel universe. As you continue this fantastic journey remember to practice. You won't be disappointed.

Do exactly what you would do if you felt most secure.
Meister Eckhart

CHAPTER SIX

When I am speaking before a group I am frequently asked the question can one trust spirit guides. True, it is especially difficult to allow your archetypal spirit guide to exert considerable influence over your life. And if you do, you may experience negativity from your family and friends who may think you are nuts or gone over to a bunch of woo-woo gibberish. Some of you may think it's heresy to even consider that a spirit guide could be untrustworthy.

Do not assume that your guides always do the right thing for you, that is for your highest good. If you are asked to give complete and implicit trust to a spirit guide a red flag should pop up. You are being asked to give up your right to choose, to make differentiations, and to be selective. Thank that guide and seek out a different one. You can specify you want a guide who respects your rights as a human being.

If you have areas of concern about the degree to which you should put your trust in a spirit guide, consider and review your intention(s). The intention is the key because it states what it is you want. As with all intentions, they should be stated in very specific language.

The late world famous psychic Sylvia Browne commented on the role of guides in changing one's "charts." By this, she was referencing one's life pattern and her comment is relevant to our question of trust. She stated, "Think of our guides as trusted friends who unconditionally love us and go through everything with us, who encourages us, and who aren't beyond giving us a gentle but effective kick in the backside." [23]

The ultimate decision regarding the trust question regarding your spirit guides rests entirely with you. You are the final arbiter.

The Universe is then identical with the cosmic nature of man.
R. A. Schwaller de Lubicz
Nature World

CHAPTER SEVEN

How do you know if your archetypal sprit guide has contacted you? Does he or she knock on your door and ask to be let in? Does the guide yell at you in a booming voice, "Pay Attention?" All too often we ignore or dismiss subtle contacts by our spirit guides because we have been conditioned to do so. Here are several clues that you are being contacted. Heed them

1. You feel a change in the room temperature where you are located.

2. You smell an unexplained fragrance, especially when no one else is in the room with you.

3. You hear a mumbling voice and are not sure from where it is coming.

4. You suddenly see different colored lights or a rainbow appear in front of you.

5. You have a feather float down in front of you or you suddenly see one as you are outdoors walking or sitting on your deck.

6. Your spirit animal suddenly appears, an eagle flies by or lands in your yard, for example.

7. During dream time, you see and hear images. Generally, these will not be a full body image and they may be in human or animal form.

8. You may feel a cool or warm breeze against your face while you are seated watching television, reading, or listening to music.

There are always little clues that you are being visited. It may take some time and definitely patience before you are comfortable in recognizing your spirit guides' presence.

We live and are apparently controlled by the
misconceptions that the spiritual world is a world of
illusion.
George Fitts

CHAPTER EIGHT

People trying to connect to their spirit guides are frequently frustrated by their apparent lack of success. All too often, the problem revolves around two basic and fundamental area: intention and negative energy.

A spirit guide must sense a viable, well thought out, intention. By intention I mean what it is you want to bring about, that is, what do you want. You can't pretend with the Spirit World. You can't say you want to help people so please let me win the lotto. You might want to consider saying something like this: "Spirit, will changing jobs be for my highest good? or something like this, "Spirit, in your infinite wisdom, do whatever is necessary to help me get over my anger."

Remember, Spirit Guides won't knock you aside of the head to get your attention. Their response will be subtle. Look for small signs.

The second problem of connecting to your spirit guide is the presence of negative energy. You may be inundated with negative energy and it may not be your fault. You may pick up negative energy at the place of work, from stores you visit, friends' homes, or your own home. The first thing you should do is to smudge yourself with sage or a combination of sage, cedar, and or Palo Santo. Get a good grounding essential oil and put in a diffuser or place one drop on your wrist and rub your wrists together.

Perhaps you home or the apartment in which you live is situated in an area that has been contaminated. In the home, television, radio, microwaves, cellphones, electric stoves and ovens may add to the negative energy in your home.

What can you do? I recommend the following: Using a quart glass jar, fill it 1/3 full of sea salt, 1/3 water, and 1/3 white vinegar. Hide the glass jar for 24 hours. When you retrieve it, if there are bubbles or a haze in the water you have negative energy.

In that case, smudge your whole house with a sage bundle, going from room to room, closets included. If you have a basement, smudge that or a crawl space under your house, waft the smoke in there. Do the same if you have an attic or upper level crawl space.

It may be necessary to do this for three or four days. At the end of that time, a simple thing you can do to check the negativity is to use a dosing rod, walk thorough each room and area. If the rod swing back and forth at a good clip, you still have negative energy. Watch where the rod points. It is really moving, that's a source of negative energy. Place some sea salt in that area or a couple of clear quartz crystals.

You can easily make a dosing rod. Take a wire coat hanger, cut out the straight bar, bend it slightly at one end. Insert that end into a straw. Hold the rod between your thumb and forefinger. Don't squeeze it. If you don't want to take the time to make one, you can buy them on Amazon.com.

SUMMARY

Patience and a willingness to change are key elements to a successful activation of your Spirit Guide(s). The old adage, *practice makes perfect* is true. Remember meeting your archetypal spirit will not happen overnight. You have to be willing to spend time, concentrated time. To release your archetypal spirit guide, to accept guidance, help, wisdom, and instruction do the following:

1. Get into a relaxed mode.
2. Imagine yourself becoming more and more relaxed, almost super casual. Allow yourself to float to a higher level of consciousness until you feel you are transcending reality.
3. Image yourself being bathed in a wonderful radiance, secure, and comfortable.
4. Visualize your archetypal spirit guide.
5. Feel the space that surrounds the two of you.
6. Imagine your archetypal spirit guide coming close to you. Join with him or her as you are welcomed into a higher realm. Feel the wonderful, tingling vibrations surrounding you.
7. Sit silently. Listen. Let impressions come to you. Be accepting. Look at your guide. Notice specific features such as his or her eyes. Feel with your whole being. Do not judge or censor any of these sensations. Simply accept them as they are.
8. Ask your archetypal spirit guide if he or she has a message for you. It may be specific or it may be a symbol. Listen and look.

9. When you have the message or symbol, acknowledge it and thank your guide. Slowly come back to your place.

10. Relax for a few minutes. Don't move. Just stall still. Gradually begin to think about your message or symbol, and about the experience you just had. Allow them to sink in. Then get up, jot down a few notes about the experience, and go about your daily routine.

11. When you have time, later in the day, sit down, relax, look over your notes and call back your experience, the received message or symbol. Think about each. Jot down a few comments about your message or symbol, or your encounter so you can come back to them again later. This is important for clarity of the message.

Carl Jung did just that as he searched for the meanings of his own symbols.

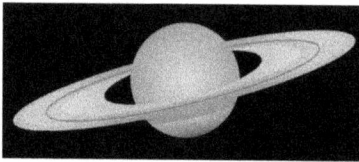

Rejoice at small gains; don't be impatient, as impatience hampers growth.
Mildred Lisette Norman
Quoted in *The Book of Answers.* [24]
by Carol Bolt.

BIBLIOGRAPHY

Beauregard, Mario & Denyse O'Leary. The Spiritual Brain: A Neuroscientist's Case for the Existence of the Soul. New York: Harper One, 2007.

Beauregard, Mario. Brain Wars. New York: Harper One, 2013.

Begley, Sharon. Train Your Mind Change Your Brain. New York: Ballantine Books, 2007.

Davich, Victor, N. 8 Minute Meditation: Quiet Your Mind. New York: Perigee Trade, 2004.

Gunaratano, Bhate Henepola. Mindfulness In Plain English, Revised, and Expanded Edition. Somerville: Wisdom Publications, 1996.

Hillman, James. Archetypal Psycho log. A Brief Account. Dallas: Spring Publications, Inc. 1981.

Jaynes, Julian. The Origin of consciousness in the Breakdown of the Bicameral Mind. Boston: Houghton-Mifflin Company, 1990.

Jung, C. G. The Archetypes, and the Collective Unconscious. Princeton: Princeton University Press, 10th Printing, 1990.

Jung, C. G. Man and His Symbols. New York: Dell Publishing Company, 1964.

Jung, C. G. Psychological Types, Revised R. F. C. Hull H. G. Baynes Translation. Princeton: Princeton University Press, 1971.

Jung, C. G. Four Archetypes: Mother, Rebirth, Spirit, Trickster. R. F. C. Hull, Translation. Princeton: Princeton University Press, 1973.

Jung, Emma. Animus and Anima. Dallas: Spring Publications, 1958.

Kaku, Michio. Parallel Worlds. New York. Anchor Books, 2005.

Keirsey, David. Portraits of Temperament. Del Mar: Gnosology Books, Ltd. 1989.

Ingerman, Sandra. Shamanic Journeying A Beginner's Guide. Boulder, CO. Sounds True, 2008.

Langford, Michael. The Most Direct Means of Eternal Bliss, 2008.

Oldman, John M and Lois B. Moris. Personality Self-Portrait. New York: Bantam Books. 1990.

Pearson, Carol S. The Hero Within: Six Archetypes We Live By. New York: Harper Row, 199.

Ridal, Kathryn. How to Reach Out to Your Spirit guides. Toronto; Bantam Books, 1988.

Roman, Sanaya and Duane Packer. Opening to Channel: How to Connect with Your Inner Guide. Tiburon: H. J. Kramer, Inc. 1987.

Schuman, Sandra G. Source Imagery: Releasing the Power of Your Creativity. New York. Doubleday, 1989.

Stanton, Marian. Archetypal Psychologies: Reflections in Honor of James Hillman. New Orleans: Spring Journal Publications, 2008.

Wilber, Ken. No Boundary. Boston: Shambhala, 2001.

Yarbroff, William. The Inner Image: A Resource for Type Development. Palo Alto: Consulting Psychologists Press, Inc. 1990.

Yogani. Deep Meditations: Pathway to Personal Freedom. Jacksonville: AYP Publishing, 2005.

ENDNOTES

Refer to [] within the body of the text

Dr. Paul Reber, "What is the Memory Capacity of the Human Brain." Scientific American, June, 2010.

Mana is a spiritual quality of supernatural origin; a sacred force existing in the universe.

"The Enfolding-Unfolding Universe: A Conversation with David Bohm" by Renee Weber in *The Holographic Paradigm.* Ken Wilber, ed. Boulder. New Science Library, 1982, p. 72.

C. G. Jung. The Archetypes and the Collective Unconscious. New York. Princeton University Press, 10th Printing. 1990, p. 156.Mark Schorer in William Blake: The Politics of Vision. New York. Harper & Row, 1988, p. 29.

David Feinstein and Stanley Krippner. Personal Mythology. Los Angeles. Jeremy P. Tarcher, Inc. 1988, p. 241.Joseph Campbell. Historical Atlas of World Mythology, Vol 1, Part 1. New York. Harper & Row, 1988.

These steps are based on Sanaya Roman and Duane Packer's Book, *Opening to Channel; How to connect with your Guide* and Kathryn Ridall's *How to Reach Out to Your Spirit Guides*. New York. Bantam. 1988.An almond-shaped neural structure in the anterior part of the temporal lobe of the cerebrum; it plays an important role in motivation and emotional behavior.

Qi-energy in traditional Chinese culture means the active principle forming part of living things, that is, life force.

C. G. Jung. The Collected works, 1947-1954, par. 420.Jean Shinoda Bolen. Gods in Everyman: New

Psychology of Men's Lives and Loves. San Francisco. Harper Row Publishers, 1989, p. 5.

Dr. Josh Axe is a well known physician, nutritionist, author, radio host. His website: http://draxe.com/avoiding-fluoride-and-how-to-detox-it-from-your-bodyLeavy, Ashley. MimosaMario Beauregard. *Brain Wars*. New York. Harper Collins. 2012. p. 74.

Op. cit. p. 6.Activating Your Pineal gland: The Mind Unleashed. September 14, 2014.Yeha-Noha is 1994 song by Sacred Spirit, a German musical project. From the album, Chants and Dances of the Native Americans.Psychology Today Therapists, 01/28/2014.Michio Kaku. Parallel Worlds. New York. Anchor Books. 2005, 93.

Michael Talbot. The Holographic Universe. New York. Harper Collins. 1991. p. 48Quoted in The Holographic Universe. Michael Talbot. New York. Harper Collins. 1991. p. 61.Brown, Sylvia. 10 Questions Answered About Your Spirit Guides. Communicating with Your Guides. Printed on http://www.healyourlifecom Jan. 04, 2015.Carol Bolt. The Souls Book of Answers. New York. Stewart, Tabori & Chang. 2003.

www.ingramcontent.com/pod-product-compliance
Lightning Source LLC
Chambersburg PA
CBHW060427050426
42449CB00009B/2172